GRAPHIC LIBRARY™

W9-BBZ-124

GRAPHIC BIOGRAPHIES

JANE GOODALL

ANIMAL SCIENTIST

by Katherine Krohn

illustrated by Cynthia Martin
and Anne Timmons

Capstone
press

Mankato, Minnesota

Graphic Library is published by Capstone Press,
1710 Roe Crest Drive, North Mankato, Minnesota 56003.
www.capstonepub.com

Printed in the United States of America in Stevens Point, Wisconsin.
122011
006527WZVMI

Library of Congress Cataloging-in-Publication Data
Krohn, Katherine.
Jane Goodall : animal scientist / by Katherine Krohn; illustrated by Cynthia Martin and Anne Timmons.
p. cm.—(Graphic library. Graphic biographies)
Includes bibliographical references and index.
ISBN-13: 978-0-7368-5485-6 (hardcover)
ISBN-10: 0-7368-5485-1 (hardcover)
ISBN-13: 978-0-7368-6885-3 (softcover pbk.)
ISBN-10: 0-7368-6885-2 (softcover pbk.)
1. Goodall, Jane, 1934—Juvenile literature. 2. Primatologists—England—Biography—Juvenile literature. 3. Chimpanzees—Tanzania—Gombe Stream National Park—Juvenile literature. I. Title. II. Series. III. Martin, Cynthia, ill. IV. Timmons, Anne, ill.
QL31.G58K76 2006
590.92—dc22 2005031214

Summary: In graphic novel format, tells the life story of animal scientist Jane Goodall.

Art Direction and Design
Jason Knudson

Designer
Thomas Emery

Storyboard Artist
Bobbi J. Wyss

Production Designer
Alison Thiele

Colorist
Cynthia Martin

Editor
Erika L. Shores

Editor's note: Direct quotations from primary sources are indicated by a yellow background.

Direct quotations appear on the following pages:
Pages 5, 11, 27, from *My Life with the Chimpanzees* by Jane Goodall (New York: Pocket Books, 1996).
Page 6, from *The Story of Dr. Doolittle* by Hugh Lofting (New York: Fredrick A. Stokes Company, 1920).
Page 26 (top), from *The Chimpanzees I Love: Saving Their World and Ours* by Jane Goodall (New York: Scholastic, 2001).
Page 26 (bottom), as quoted in Jane Goodall's interview with CNN found at http://www.cnn.com/2005/US/02/07/cnn25.tan.goodall/

TABLE OF CONTENTS

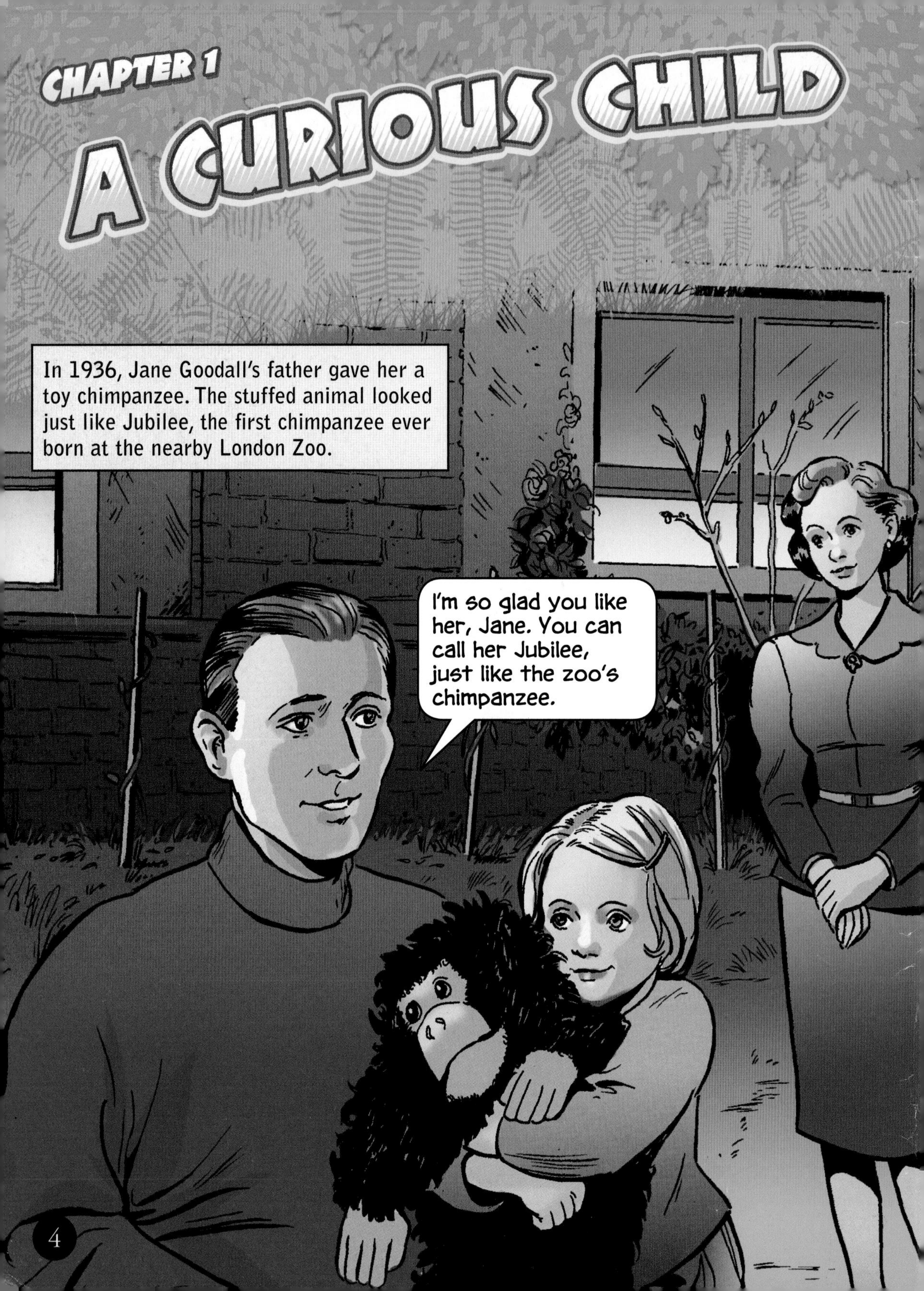
CHAPTER 1
A CURIOUS CHILD
In 1936, Jane Goodall's father gave her a toy chimpanzee. The stuffed animal looked just like Jubilee, the first chimpanzee ever born at the nearby London Zoo.
I'm so glad you like her, Jane. You can call her Jubilee, just like the zoo's chimpanzee.

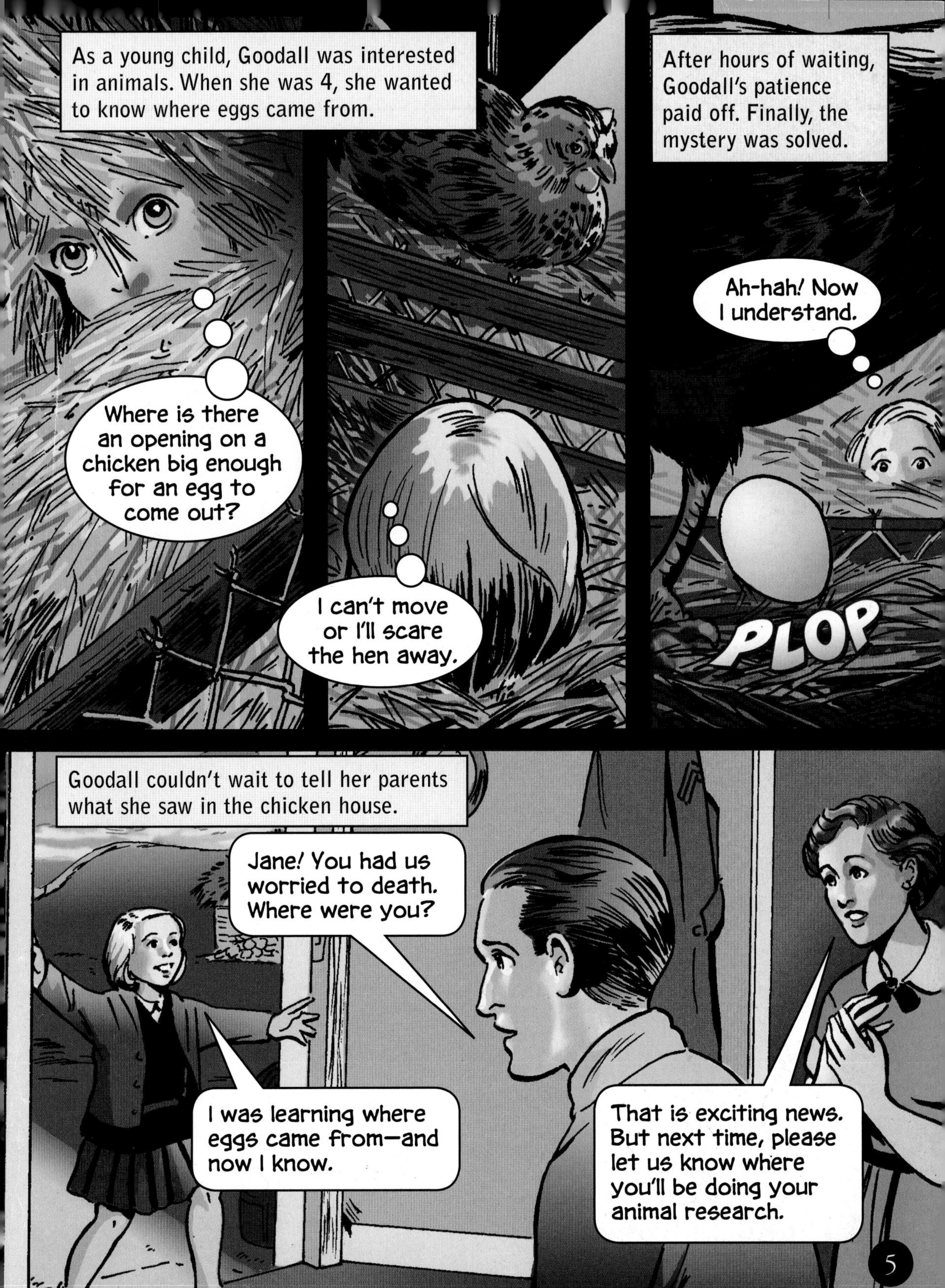
As a young child, Goodall was interested in animals. When she was 4, she wanted to know where eggs came from.
Where is there an opening on a chicken big enough for an egg to come out?
I can't move or I'll scare the hen away.
After hours of waiting, Goodall's patience paid off. Finally, the mystery was solved.
Ah-hah! Now I understand.
PLOP
Goodall couldn't wait to tell her parents what she saw in the chicken house.
Jane! You had us worried to death. Where were you?
I was learning where eggs came from—and now I know.
That is exciting news. But next time, please let us know where you'll be doing your animal research.

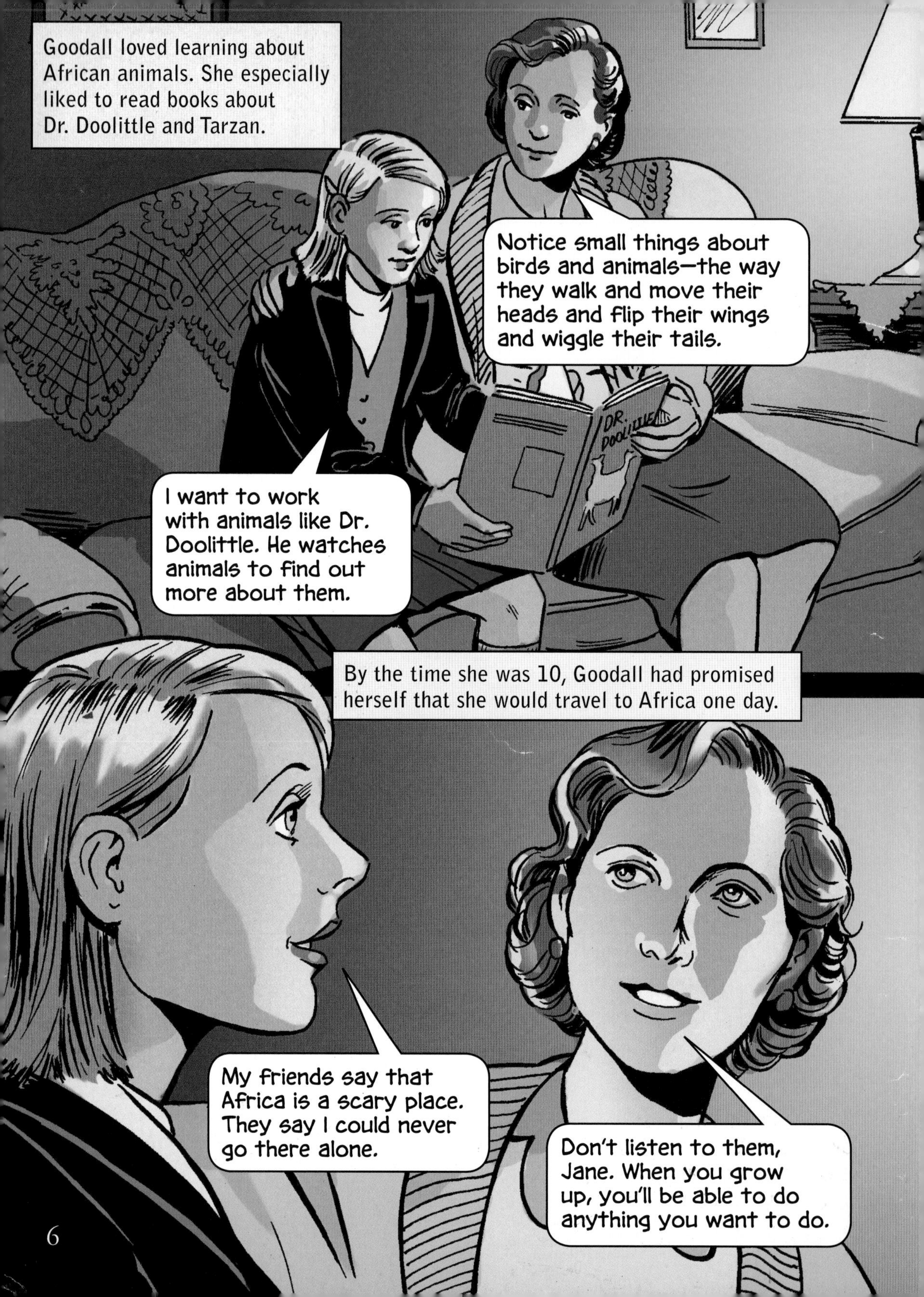
Goodall loved learning about African animals. She especially liked to read books about Dr. Doolittle and Tarzan.
Notice small things about birds and animals—the way they walk and move their heads and flip their wings and wiggle their tails.
DR. DOOLITTLE
I want to work with animals like Dr. Doolittle. He watches animals to find out more about them.
By the time she was 10, Goodall had promised herself that she would travel to Africa one day.
My friends say that Africa is a scary place. They say I could never go there alone.
Don't listen to them, Jane. When you grow up, you'll be able to do anything you want to do.

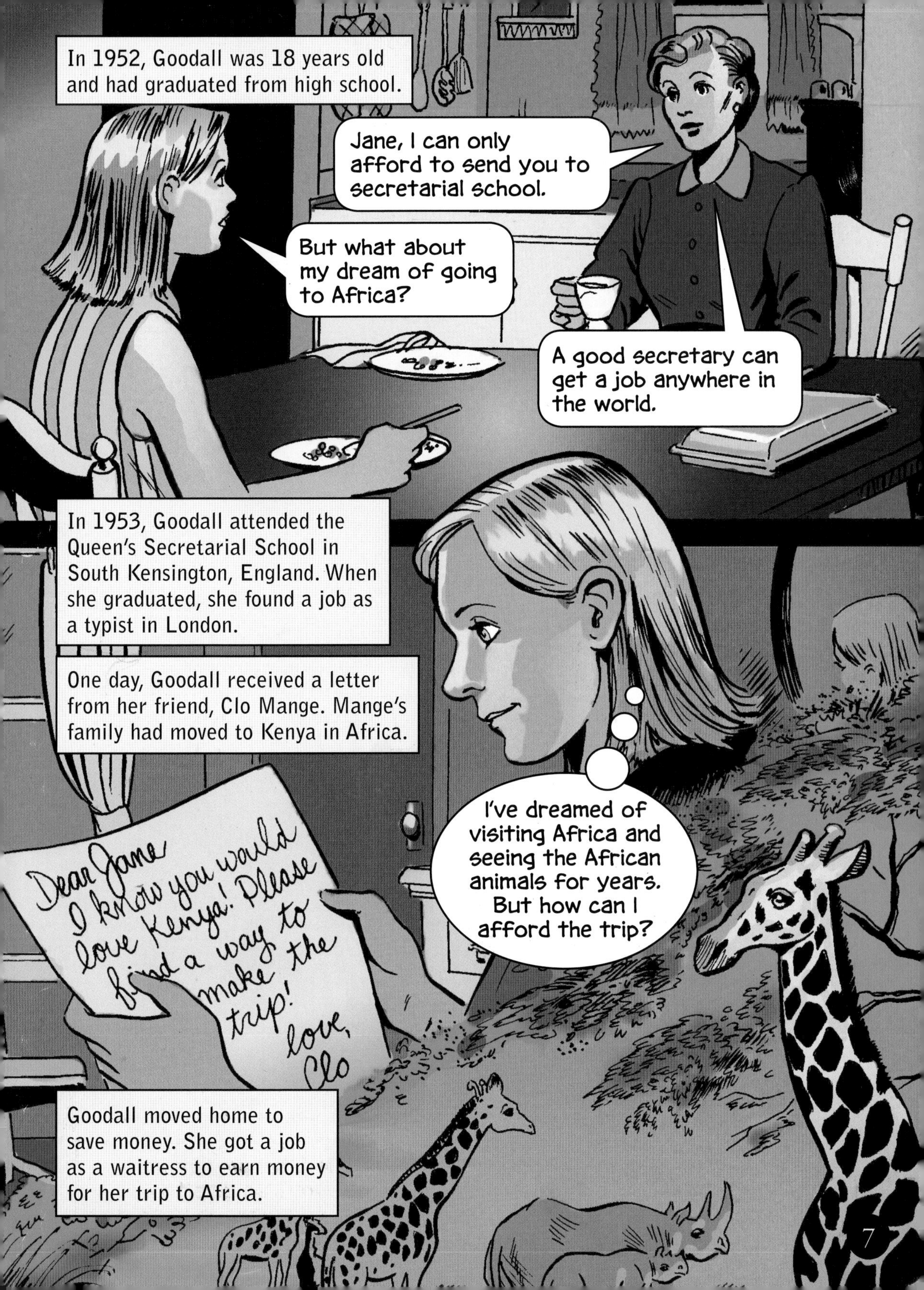

In 1952, Goodall was 18 years old and had graduated from high school.
Jane, I can only afford to send you to secretarial school.
But what about my dream of going to Africa?
A good secretary can get a job anywhere in the world.
In 1953, Goodall attended the Queen's Secretarial School in South Kensington, England. When she graduated, she found a job as a typist in London.
One day, Goodall received a letter from her friend, Clo Mange. Mange's family had moved to Kenya in Africa.
Dear Jane I know you would love Kenya! Please find a way to make the trip! love, Clo
I've dreamed of visiting Africa and seeing the African animals for years. But how can I afford the trip?
Goodall moved home to save money. She got a job as a waitress to earn money for her trip to Africa.

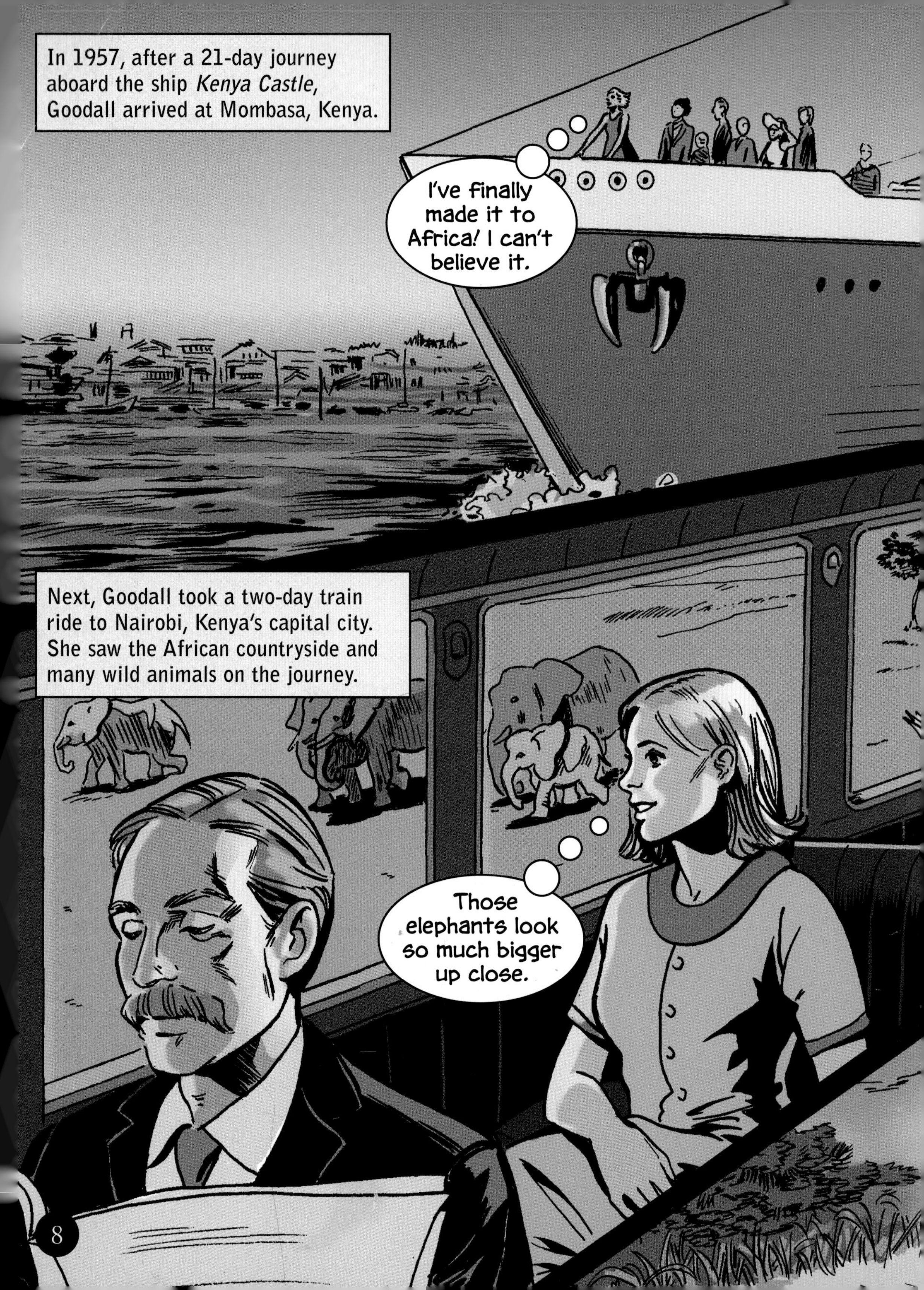
In 1957, after a 21-day journey aboard the ship *Kenya Castle*, Goodall arrived at Mombasa, Kenya.
I've finally made it to Africa! I can't believe it.
Next, Goodall took a two-day train ride to Nairobi, Kenya's capital city. She saw the African countryside and many wild animals on the journey.
Those elephants look so much bigger up close.

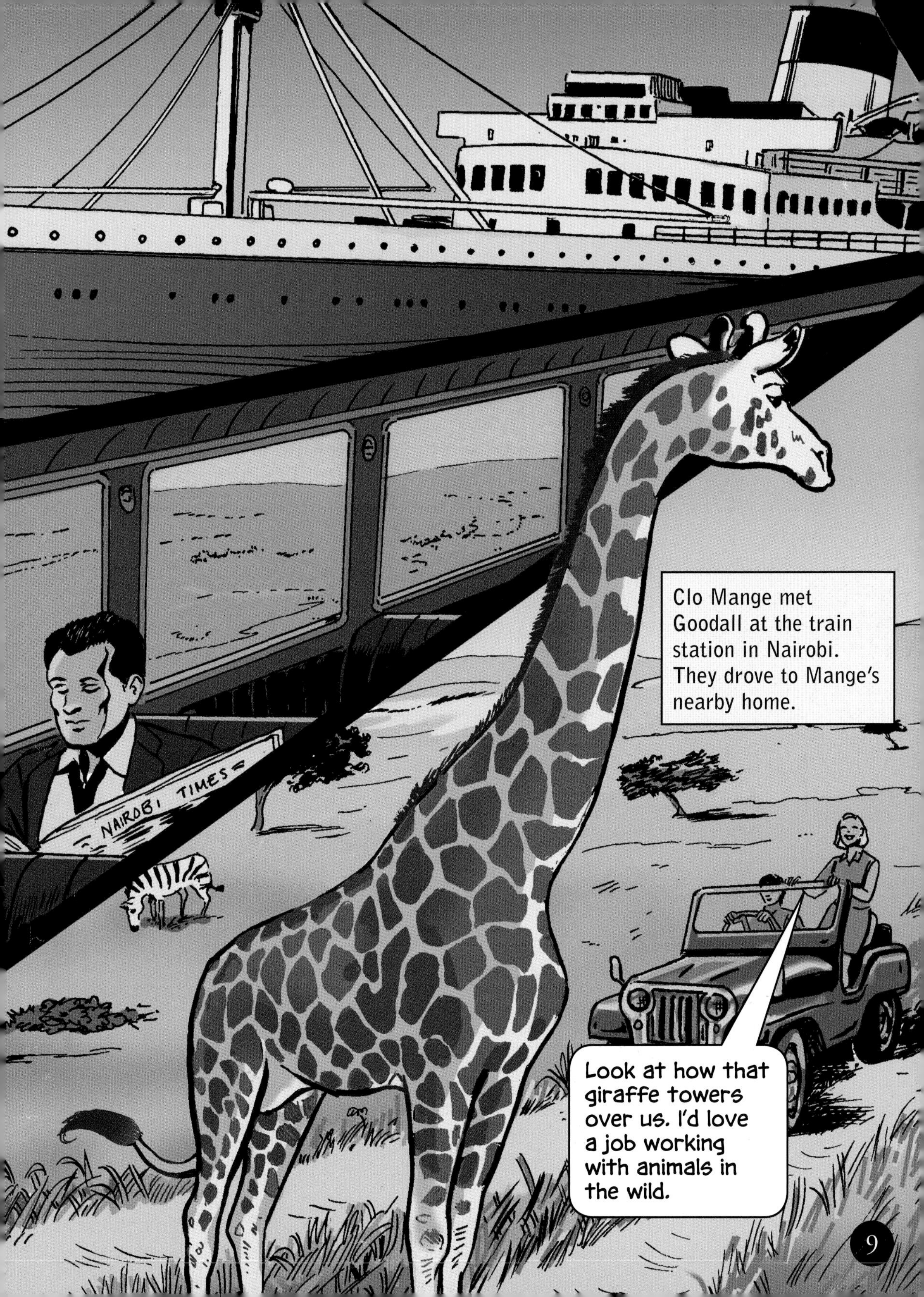
NAIROBI TIMES
Clo Mange met Goodall at the train station in Nairobi. They drove to Mange's nearby home.
Look at how that giraffe towers over us. I'd love a job working with animals in the wild.

CHAPTER 2
WORKING WITH LEAKEY

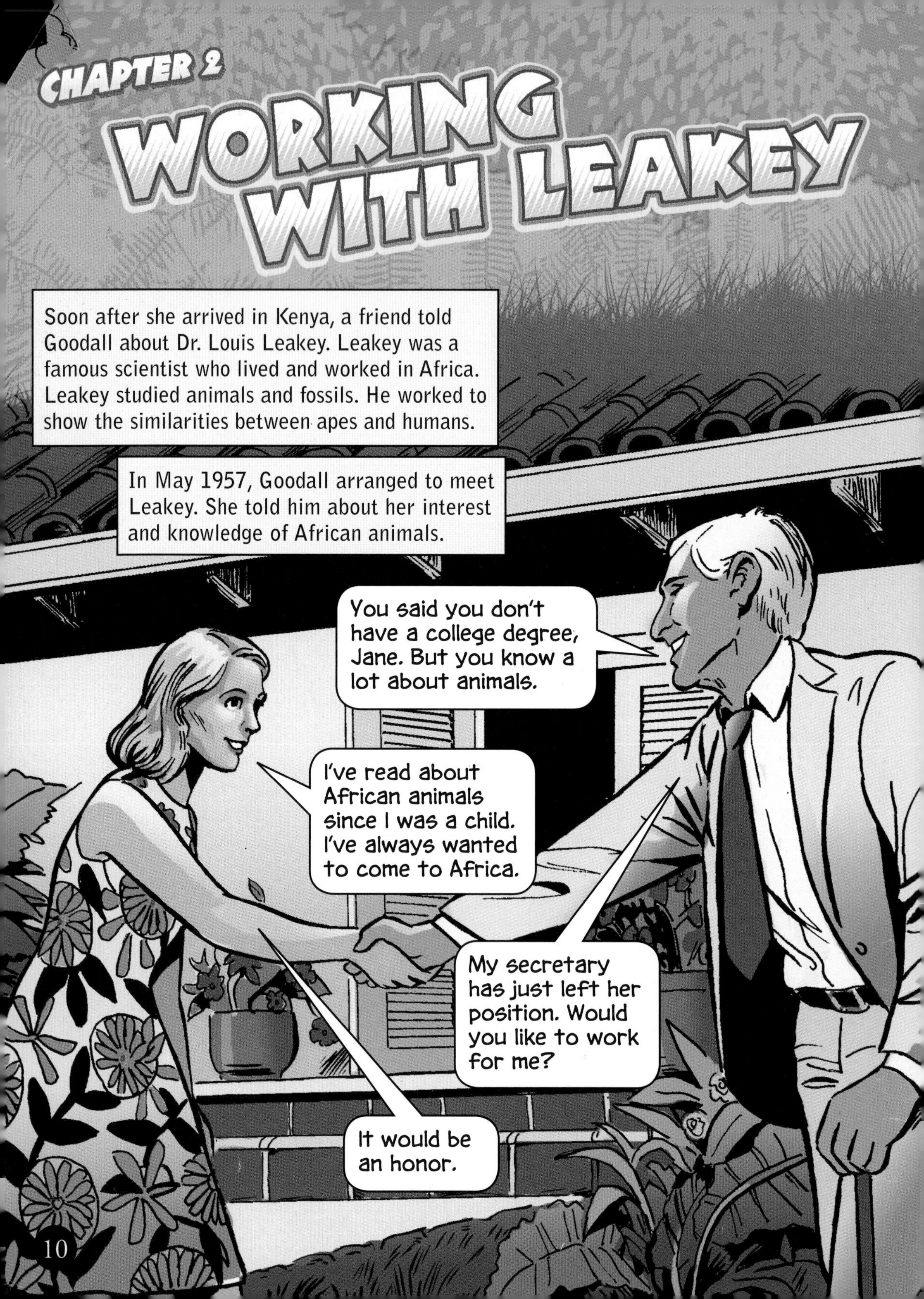
Soon after she arrived in Kenya, a friend told Goodall about Dr. Louis Leakey. Leakey was a famous scientist who lived and worked in Africa. Leakey studied animals and fossils. He worked to show the similarities between apes and humans.
In May 1957, Goodall arranged to meet Leakey. She told him about her interest and knowledge of African animals.
You said you don't have a college degree, Jane. But you know a lot about animals.
I've read about African animals since I was a child. I've always wanted to come to Africa.
My secretary has just left her position. Would you like to work for me?
It would be an honor.

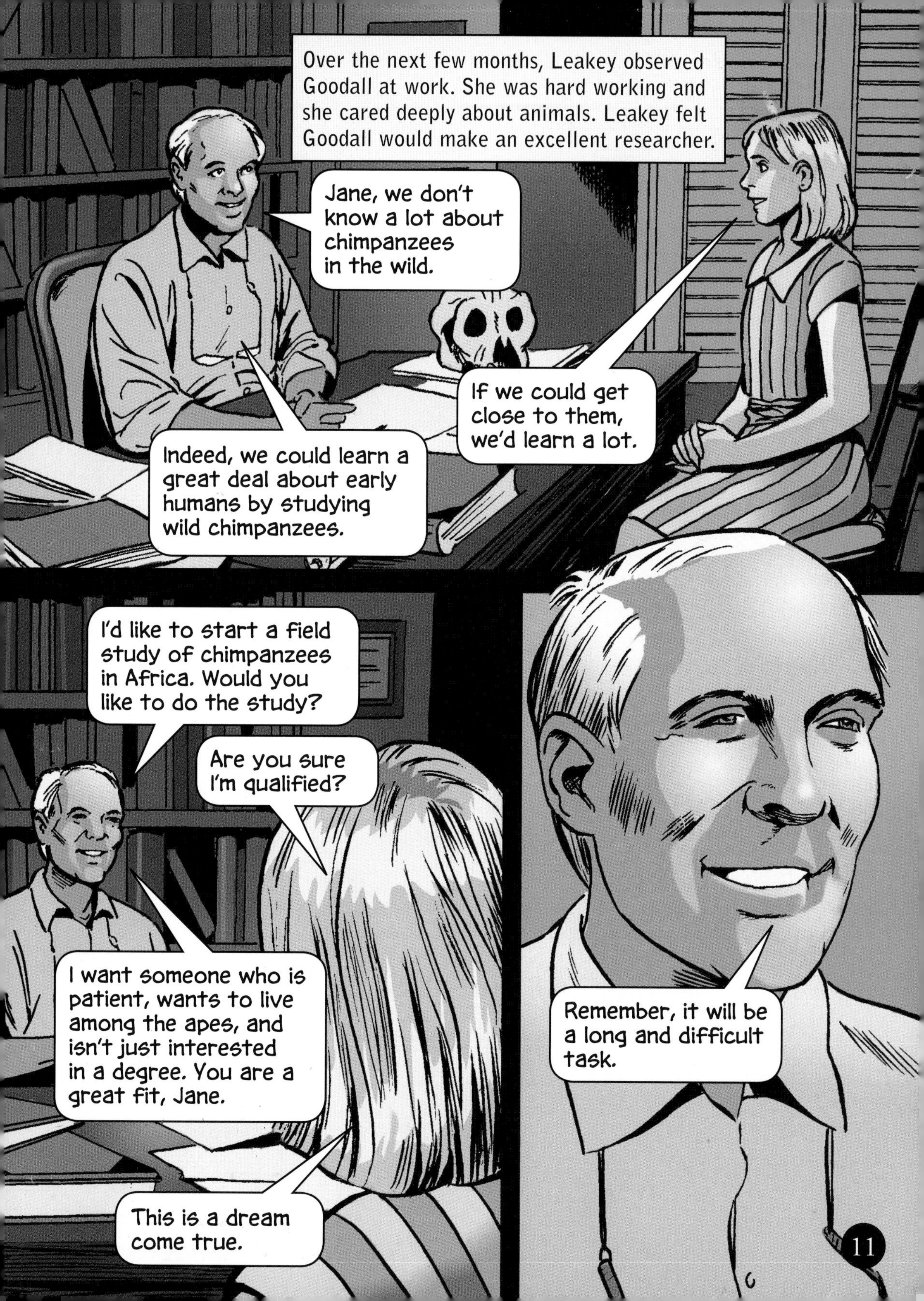

Over the next few months, Leakey observed Goodall at work. She was hard working and she cared deeply about animals. Leakey felt Goodall would make an excellent researcher.
Jane, we don't know a lot about chimpanzees in the wild.
If we could get close to them, we'd learn a lot.
Indeed, we could learn a great deal about early humans by studying wild chimpanzees.
I'd like to start a field study of chimpanzees in Africa. Would you like to do the study?
Are you sure I'm qualified?
I want someone who is patient, wants to live among the apes, and isn't just interested in a degree. You are a great fit, Jane.
This is a dream come true.
Remember, it will be a long and difficult task.

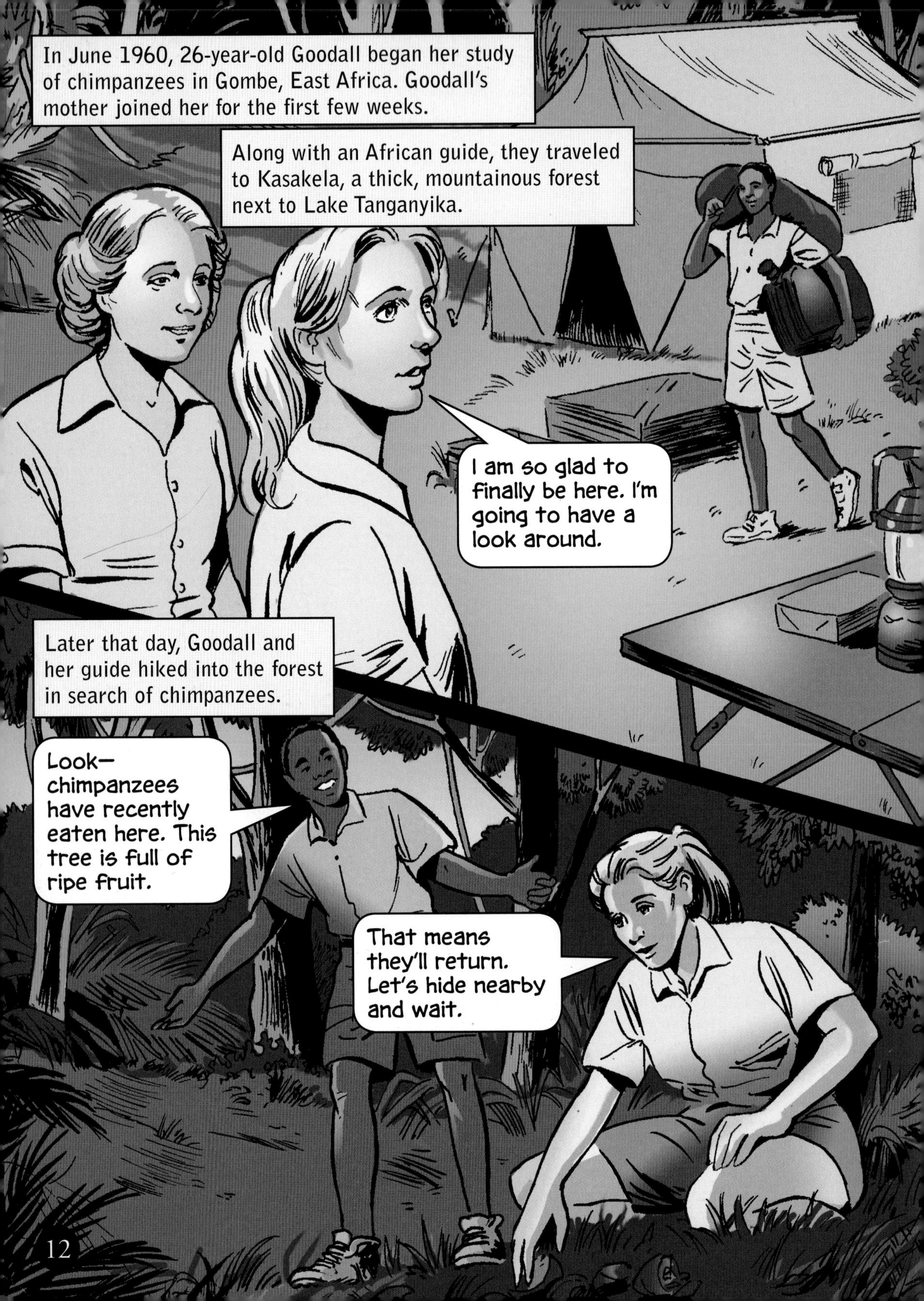
In June 1960, 26-year-old Goodall began her study of chimpanzees in Gombe, East Africa. Goodall's mother joined her for the first few weeks.
Along with an African guide, they traveled to Kasakela, a thick, mountainous forest next to Lake Tanganyika.
I am so glad to finally be here. I'm going to have a look around.
Later that day, Goodall and her guide hiked into the forest in search of chimpanzees.
Look—chimpanzees have recently eaten here. This tree is full of ripe fruit.
That means they'll return. Let's hide nearby and wait.

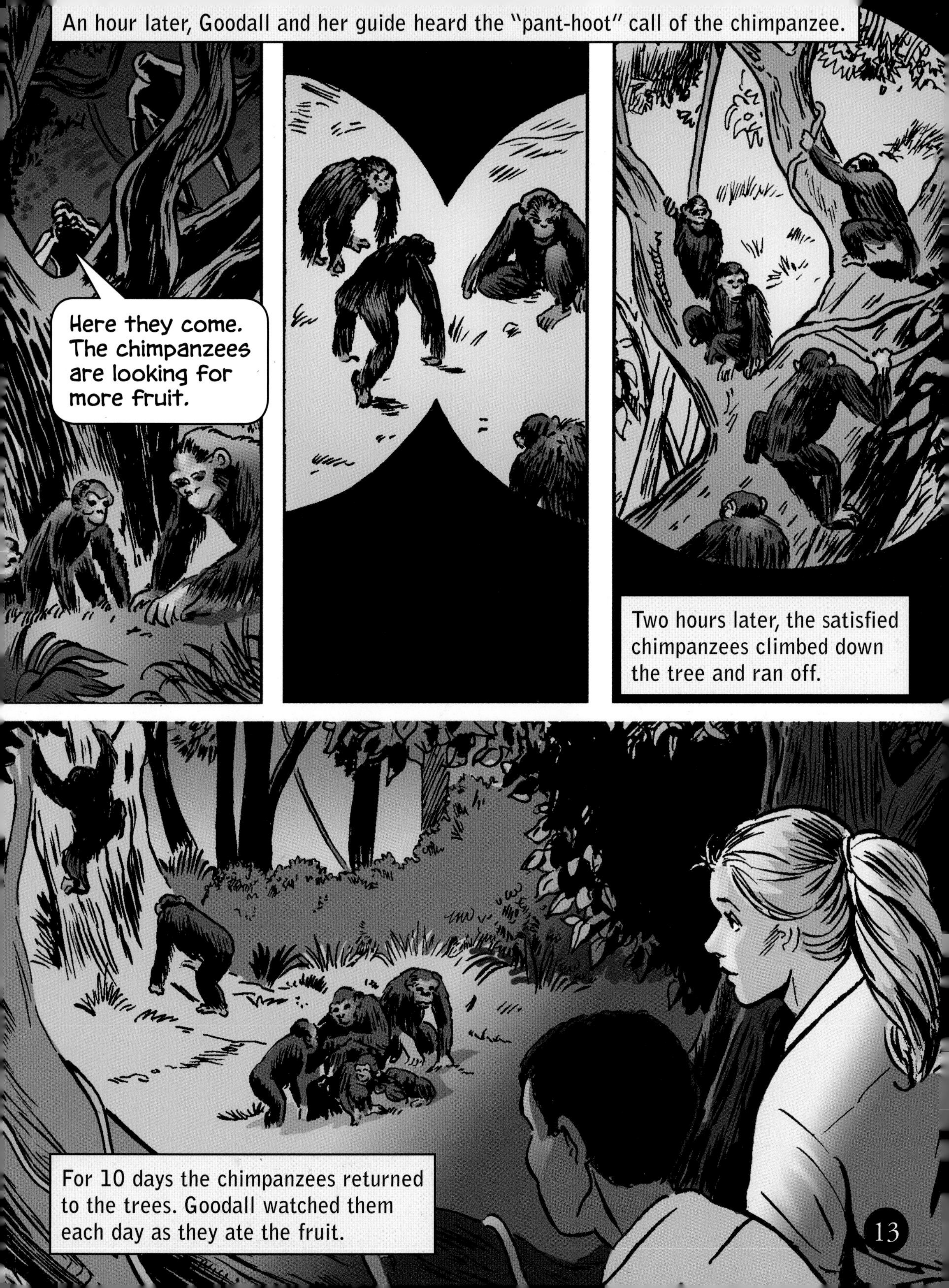
An hour later, Goodall and her guide heard the "pant-hoot" call of the chimpanzee.
Here they come. The chimpanzees are looking for more fruit.
Two hours later, the satisfied chimpanzees climbed down the tree and ran off.
For 10 days the chimpanzees returned to the trees. Goodall watched them each day as they ate the fruit.

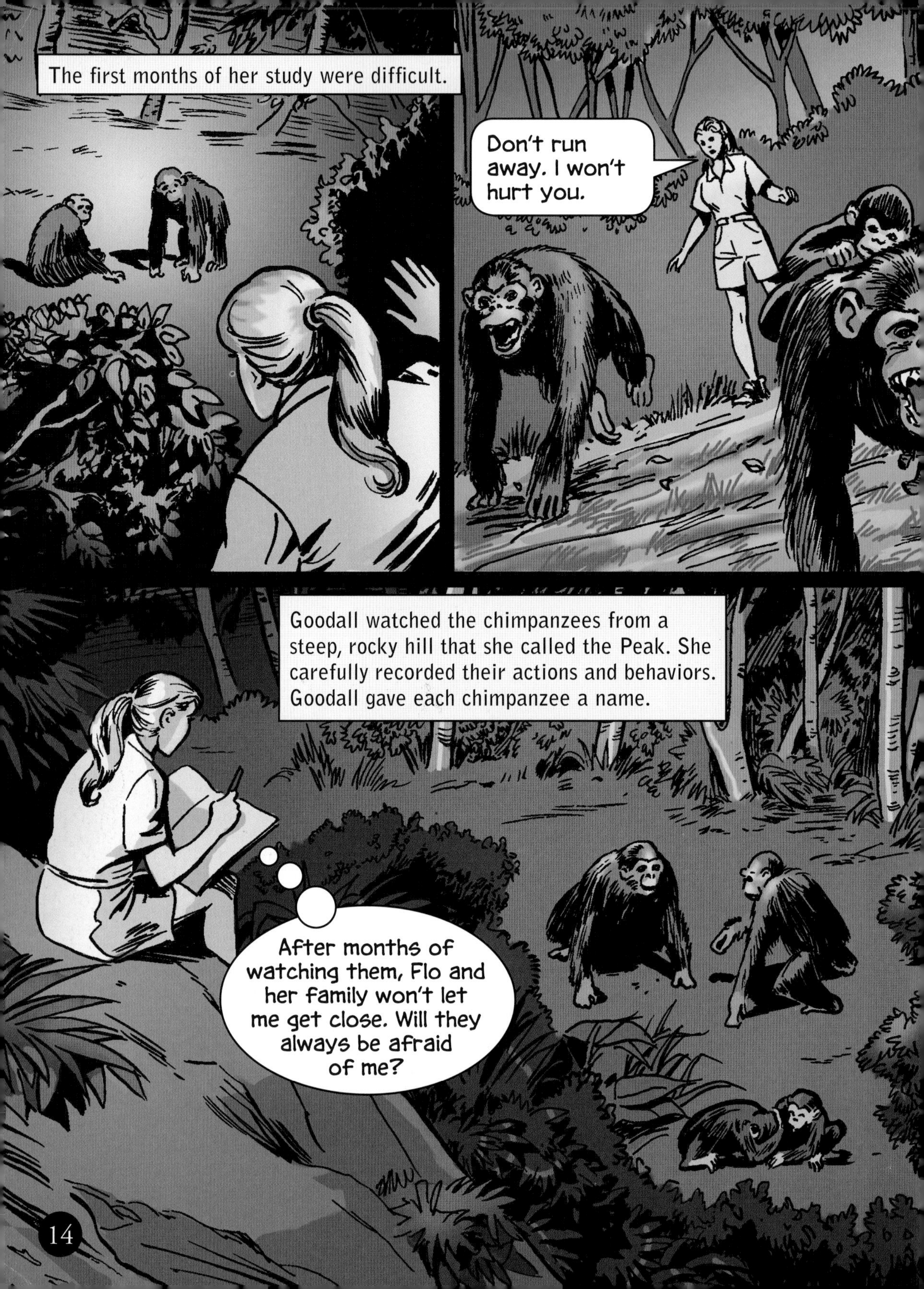
The first months of her study were difficult.
Don't run away. I won't hurt you.
Goodall watched the chimpanzees from a steep, rocky hill that she called the Peak. She carefully recorded their actions and behaviors. Goodall gave each chimpanzee a name.
After months of watching them, Flo and her family won't let me get close. Will they always be afraid of me?

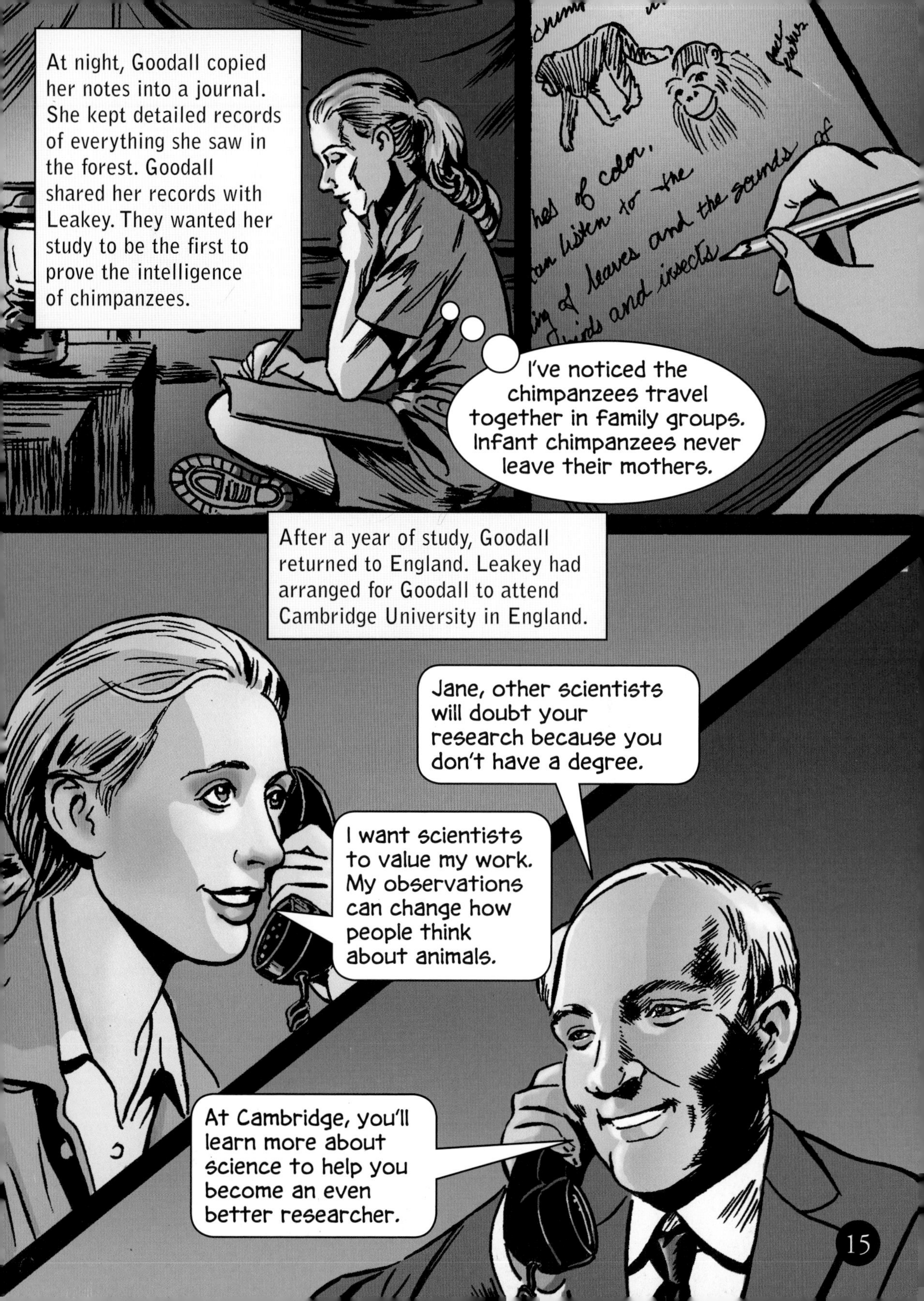

At night, Goodall copied her notes into a journal. She kept detailed records of everything she saw in the forest. Goodall shared her records with Leakey. They wanted her study to be the first to prove the intelligence of chimpanzees.
I've noticed the chimpanzees travel together in family groups. Infant chimpanzees never leave their mothers.
After a year of study, Goodall returned to England. Leakey had arranged for Goodall to attend Cambridge University in England.
Jane, other scientists will doubt your research because you don't have a degree.
I want scientists to value my work. My observations can change how people think about animals.
At Cambridge, you'll learn more about science to help you become an even better researcher.

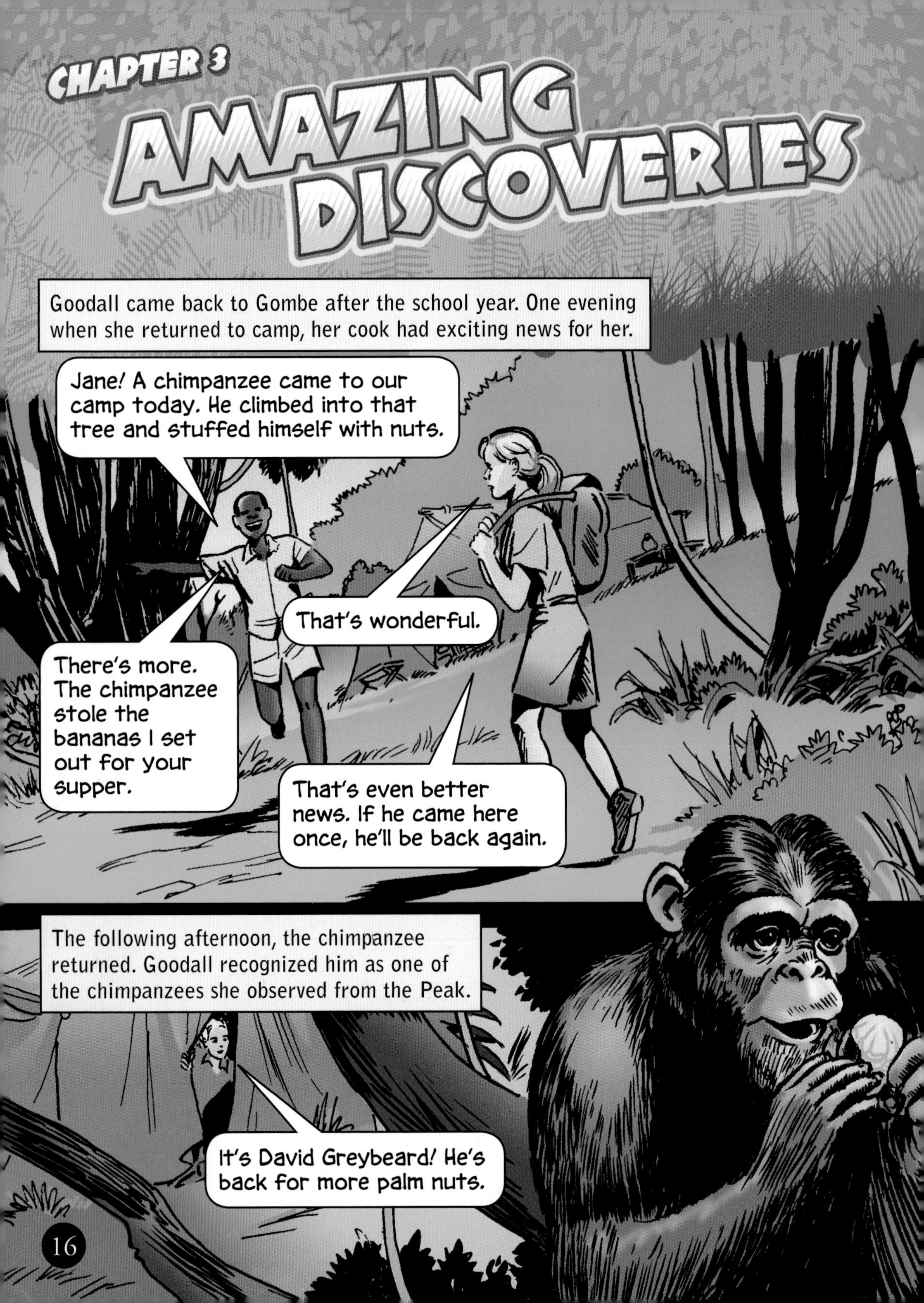
CHAPTER 3
AMAZING DISCOVERIES
Goodall came back to Gombe after the school year. One evening when she returned to camp, her cook had exciting news for her.
Jane! A chimpanzee came to our camp today. He climbed into that tree and stuffed himself with nuts.
That's wonderful.
There's more. The chimpanzee stole the bananas I set out for your supper.
That's even better news. If he came here once, he'll be back again.
The following afternoon, the chimpanzee returned. Goodall recognized him as one of the chimpanzees she observed from the Peak.
It's David Greybeard! He's back for more palm nuts.

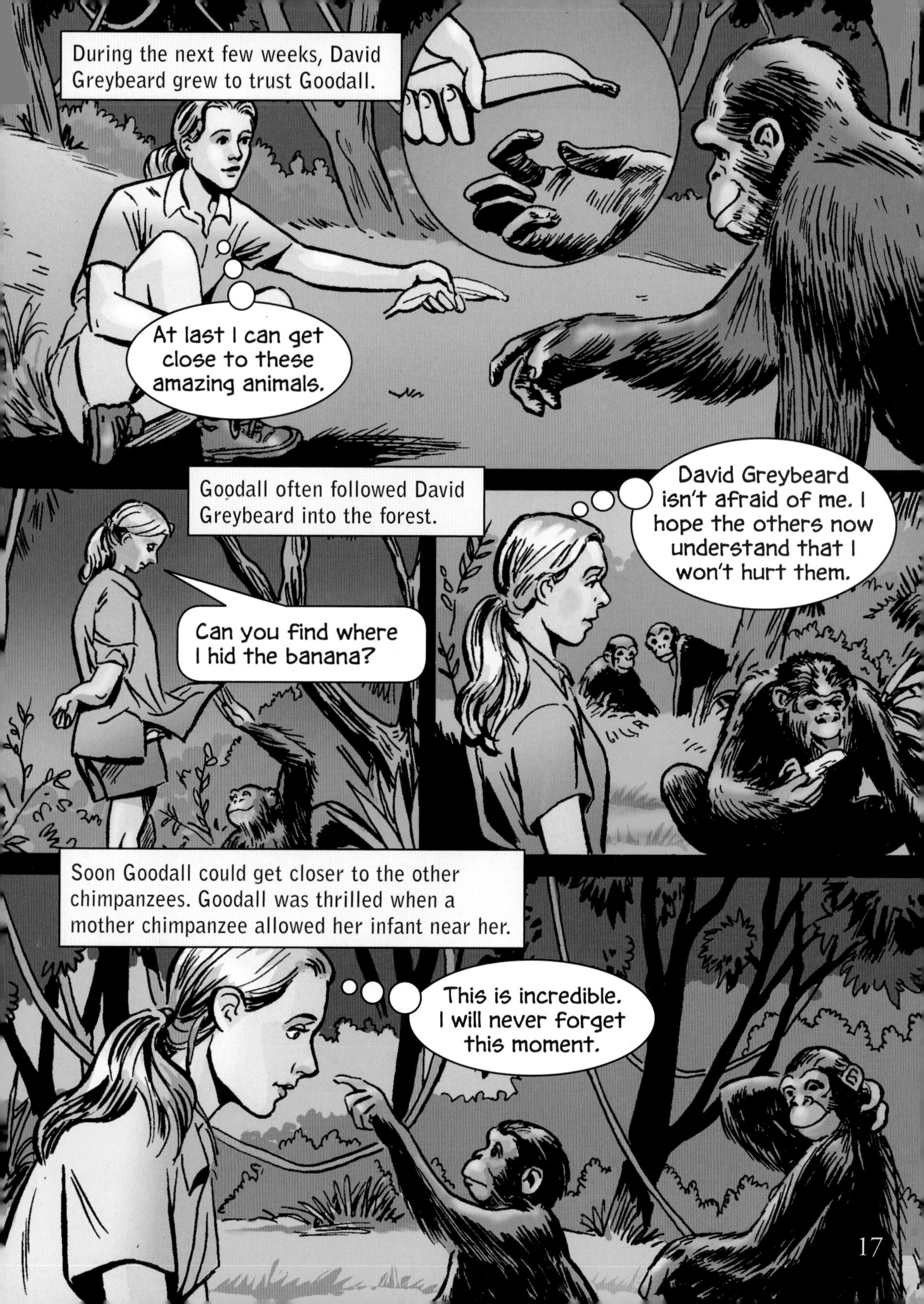

During the next few weeks, David Greybeard grew to trust Goodall.
At last I can get close to these amazing animals.
Goodall often followed David Greybeard into the forest.
Can you find where I hid the banana?
David Greybeard isn't afraid of me. I hope the others now understand that I won't hurt them.
Soon Goodall could get closer to the other chimpanzees. Goodall was thrilled when a mother chimpanzee allowed her infant near her.
This is incredible. I will never forget this moment.

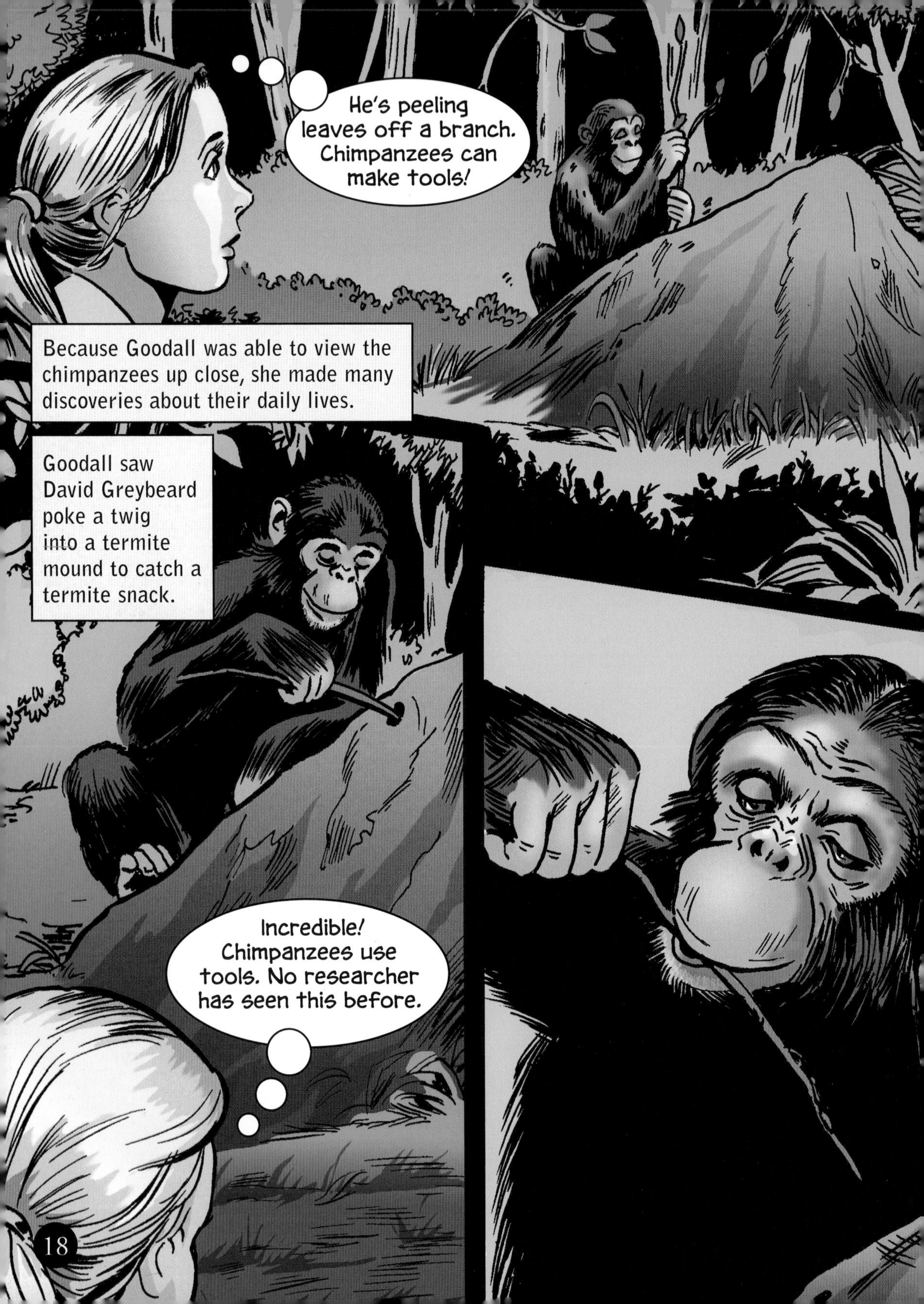
He's peeling leaves off a branch. Chimpanzees can make tools!
Because Goodall was able to view the chimpanzees up close, she made many discoveries about their daily lives.
Goodall saw David Greybeard poke a twig into a termite mound to catch a termite snack.
Incredible! Chimpanzees use tools. No researcher has seen this before.

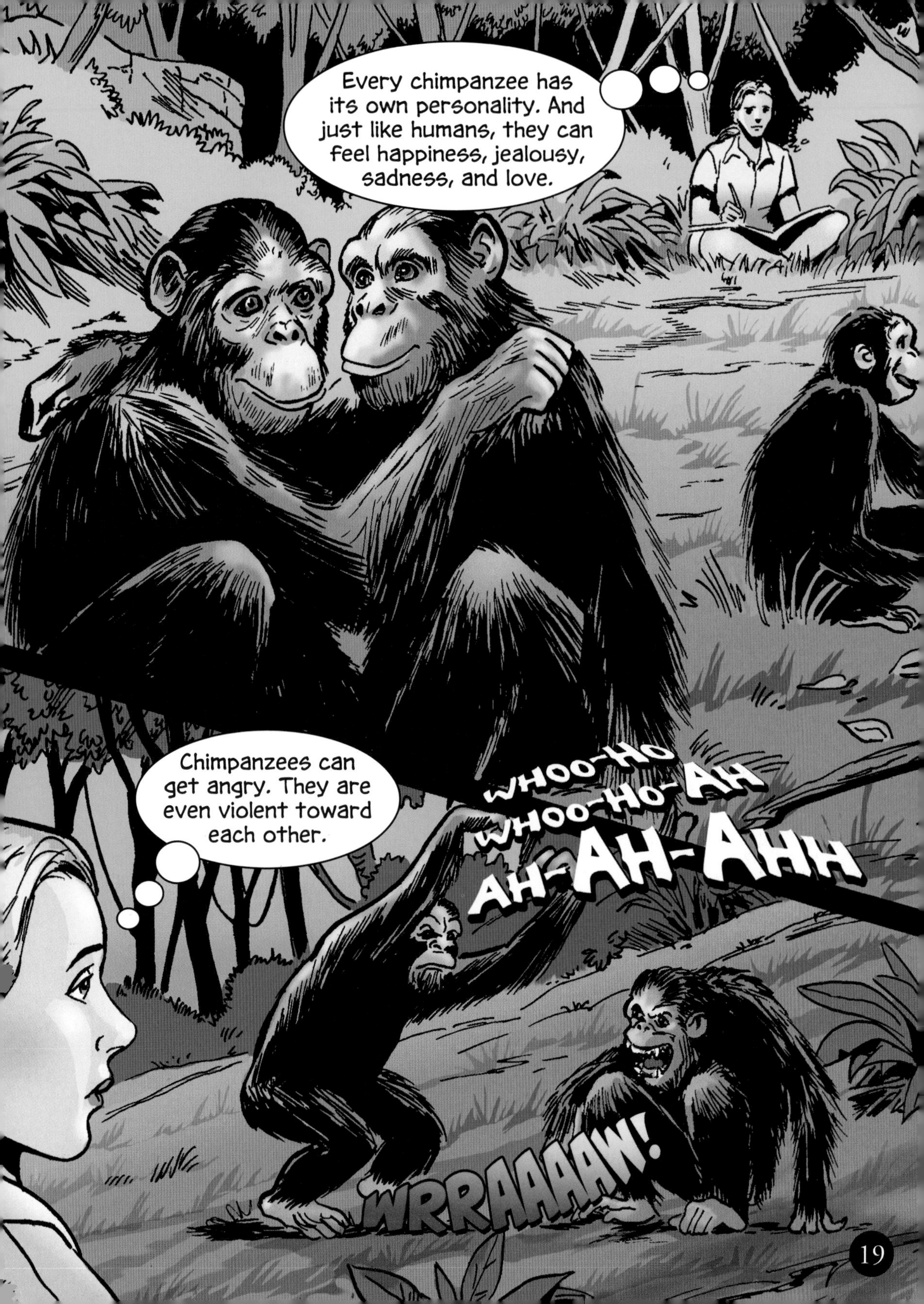
Every chimpanzee has its own personality. And just like humans, they can feel happiness, jealousy, sadness, and love.
Chimpanzees can get angry. They are even violent toward each other.
WHOO-HO
WHOO-HO-AH
AH-AH-AHH
WRRAAAAAW!

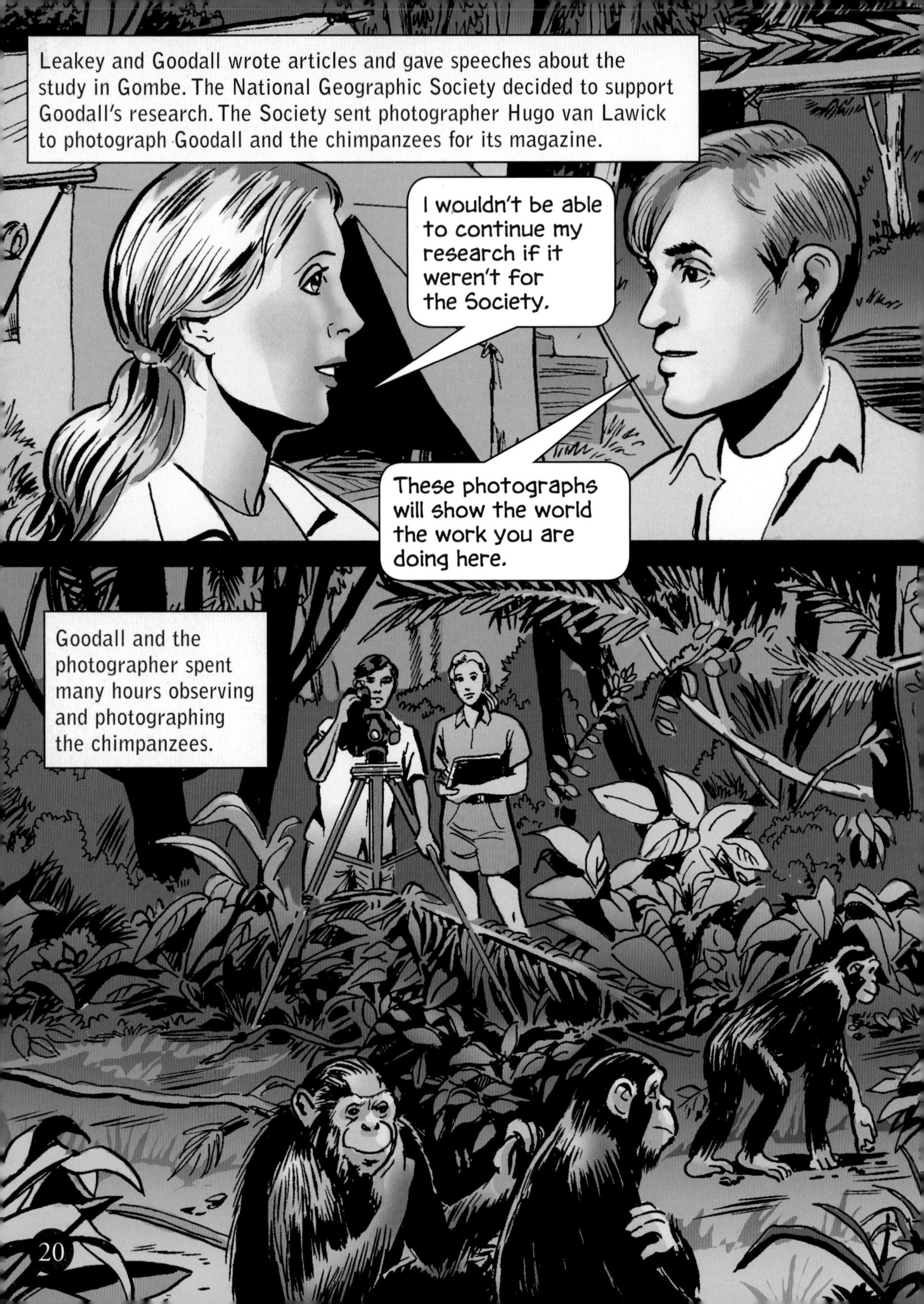
Leakey and Goodall wrote articles and gave speeches about the study in Gombe. The National Geographic Society decided to support Goodall's research. The Society sent photographer Hugo van Lawick to photograph Goodall and the chimpanzees for its magazine.
I wouldn't be able to continue my research if it weren't for the Society.
These photographs will show the world the work you are doing here.
Goodall and the photographer spent many hours observing and photographing the chimpanzees.

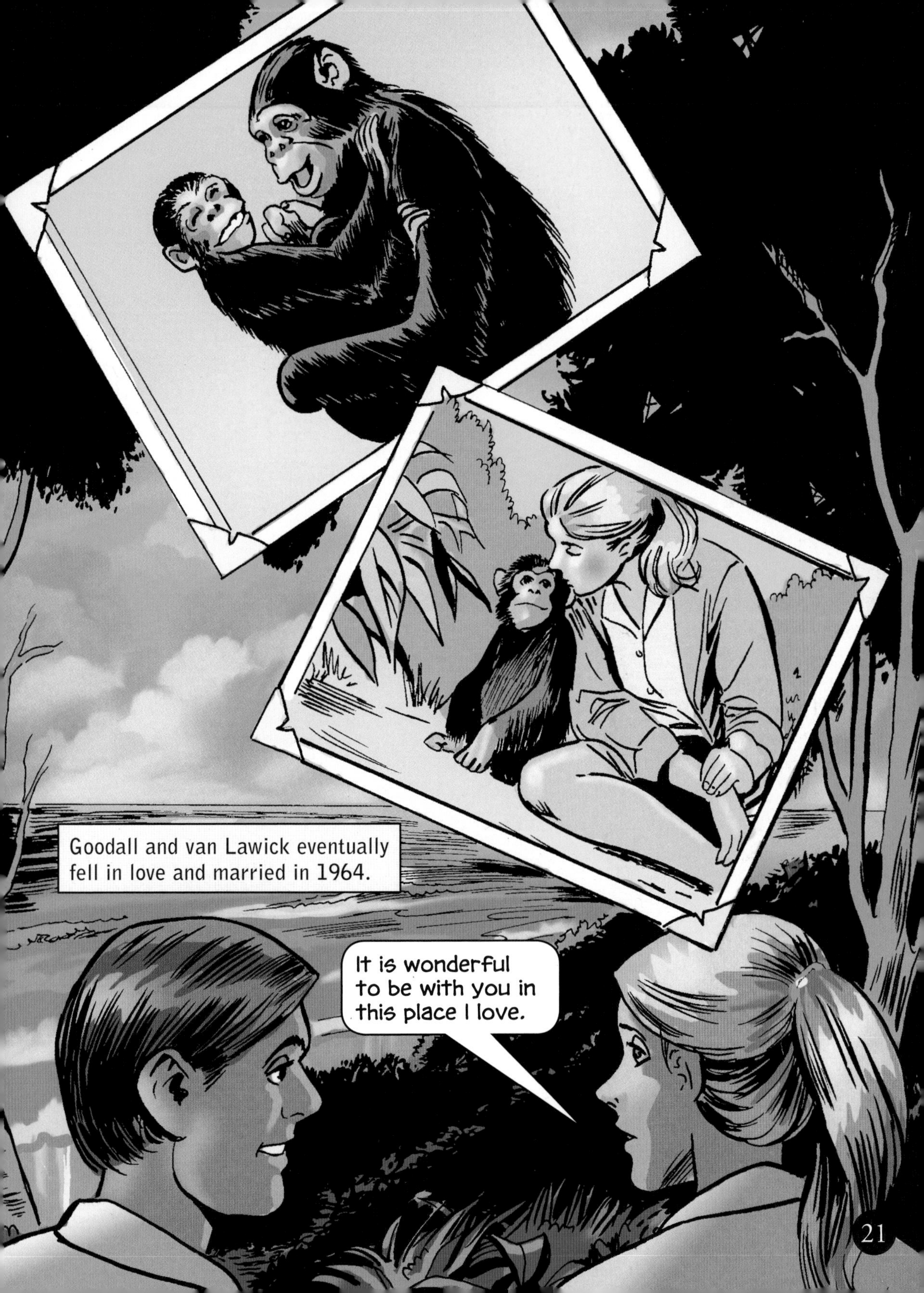
Goodall and van Lawick eventually fell in love and married in 1964.
It is wonderful to be with you in this place I love.

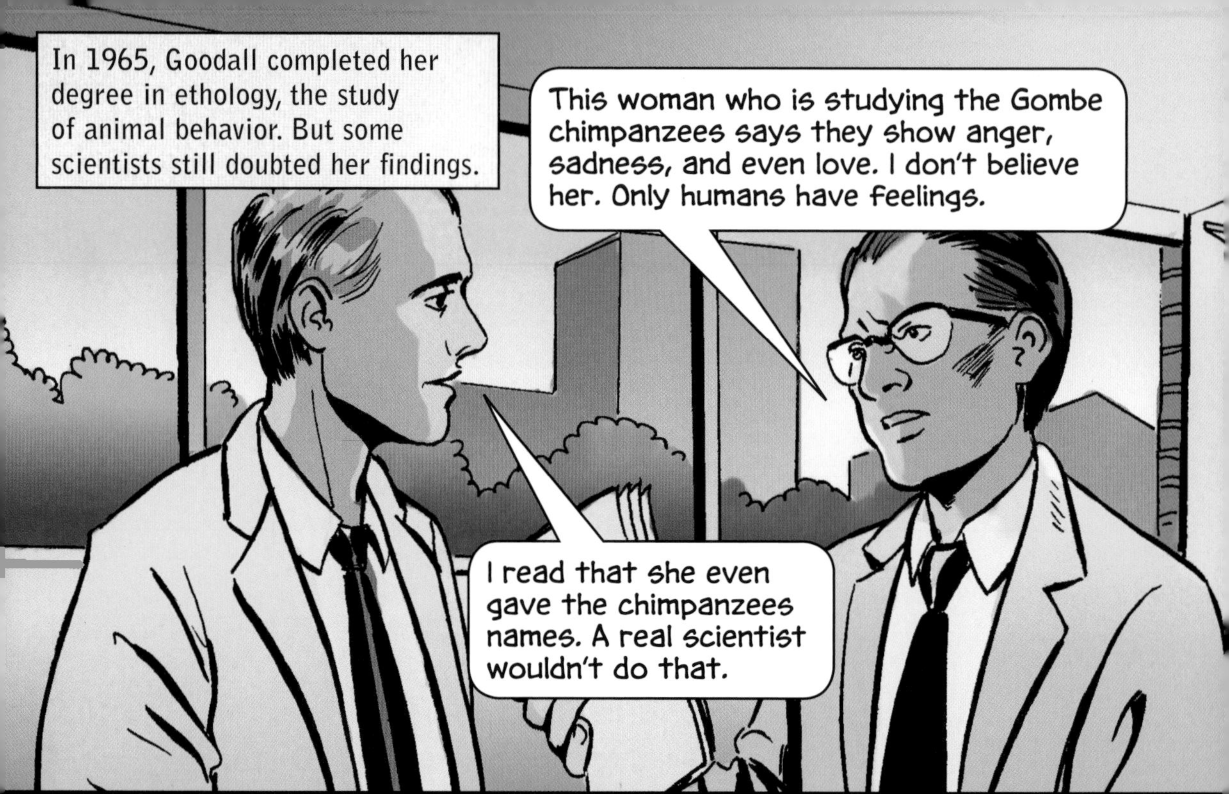
In 1965, Goodall completed her degree in ethology, the study of animal behavior. But some scientists still doubted her findings.
This woman who is studying the Gombe chimpanzees says they show anger, sadness, and even love. I don't believe her. Only humans have feelings.
I read that she even gave the chimpanzees names. A real scientist wouldn't do that.

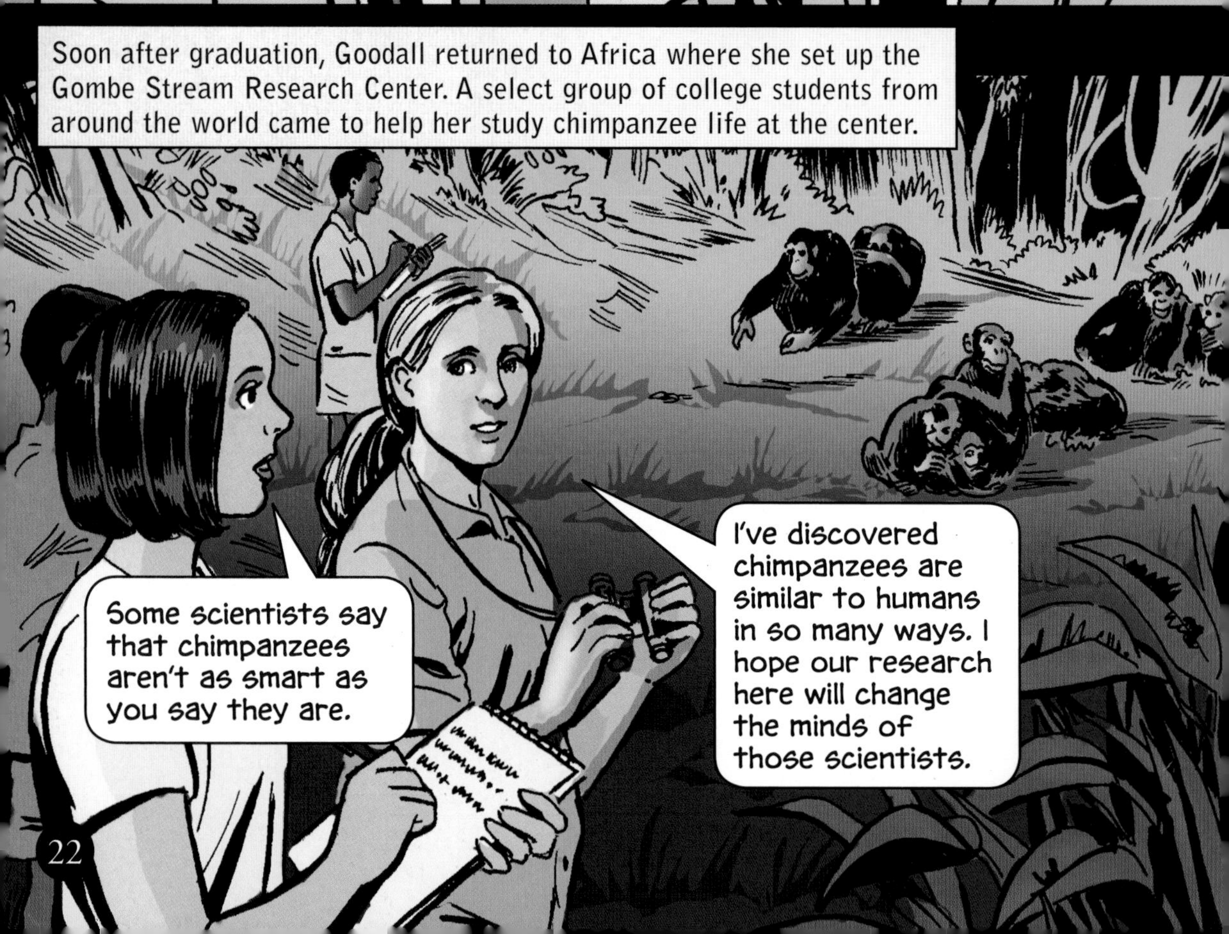
Soon after graduation, Goodall returned to Africa where she set up the Gombe Stream Research Center. A select group of college students from around the world came to help her study chimpanzee life at the center.
Some scientists say that chimpanzees aren't as smart as you say they are.
I've discovered chimpanzees are similar to humans in so many ways. I hope our research here will change the minds of those scientists.

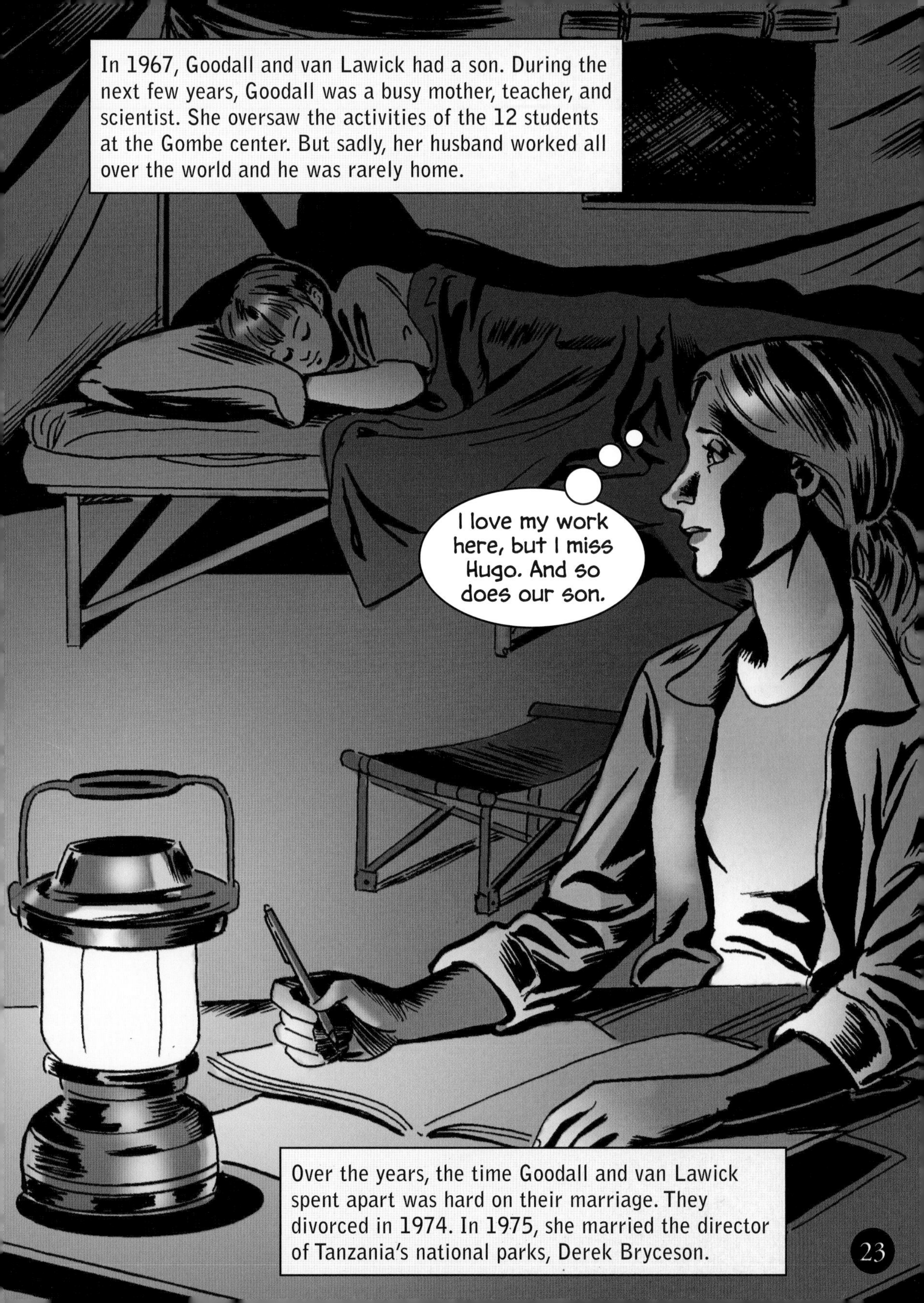
In 1967, Goodall and van Lawick had a son. During the next few years, Goodall was a busy mother, teacher, and scientist. She oversaw the activities of the 12 students at the Gombe center. But sadly, her husband worked all over the world and he was rarely home.
I love my work here, but I miss Hugo. And so does our son.
Over the years, the time Goodall and van Lawick spent apart was hard on their marriage. They divorced in 1974. In 1975, she married the director of Tanzania's national parks, Derek Bryceson.

CHAPTER 4
SHARING HER WORK

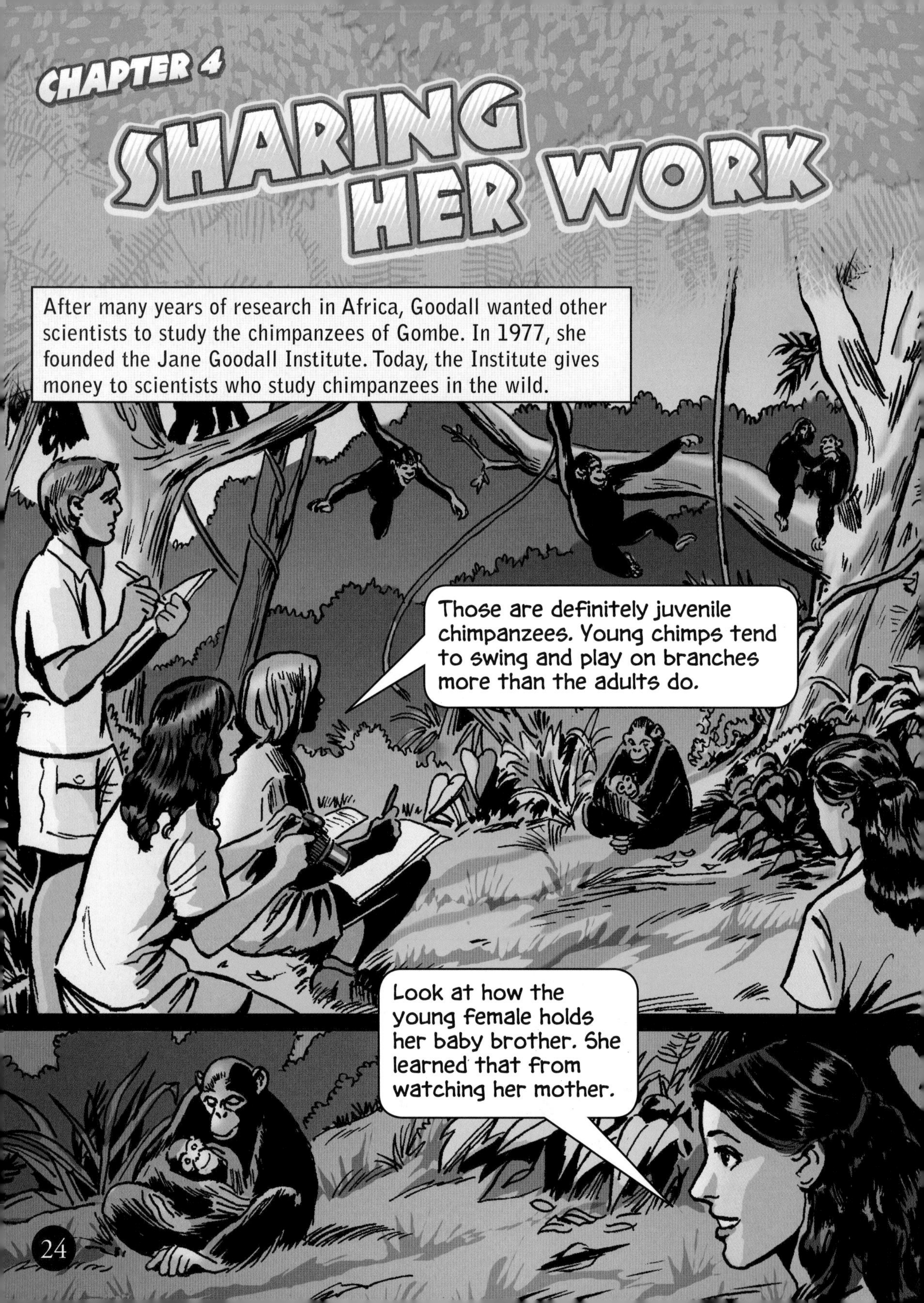
After many years of research in Africa, Goodall wanted other scientists to study the chimpanzees of Gombe. In 1977, she founded the Jane Goodall Institute. Today, the Institute gives money to scientists who study chimpanzees in the wild.
Those are definitely juvenile chimpanzees. Young chimps tend to swing and play on branches more than the adults do.
Look at how the young female holds her baby brother. She learned that from watching her mother.

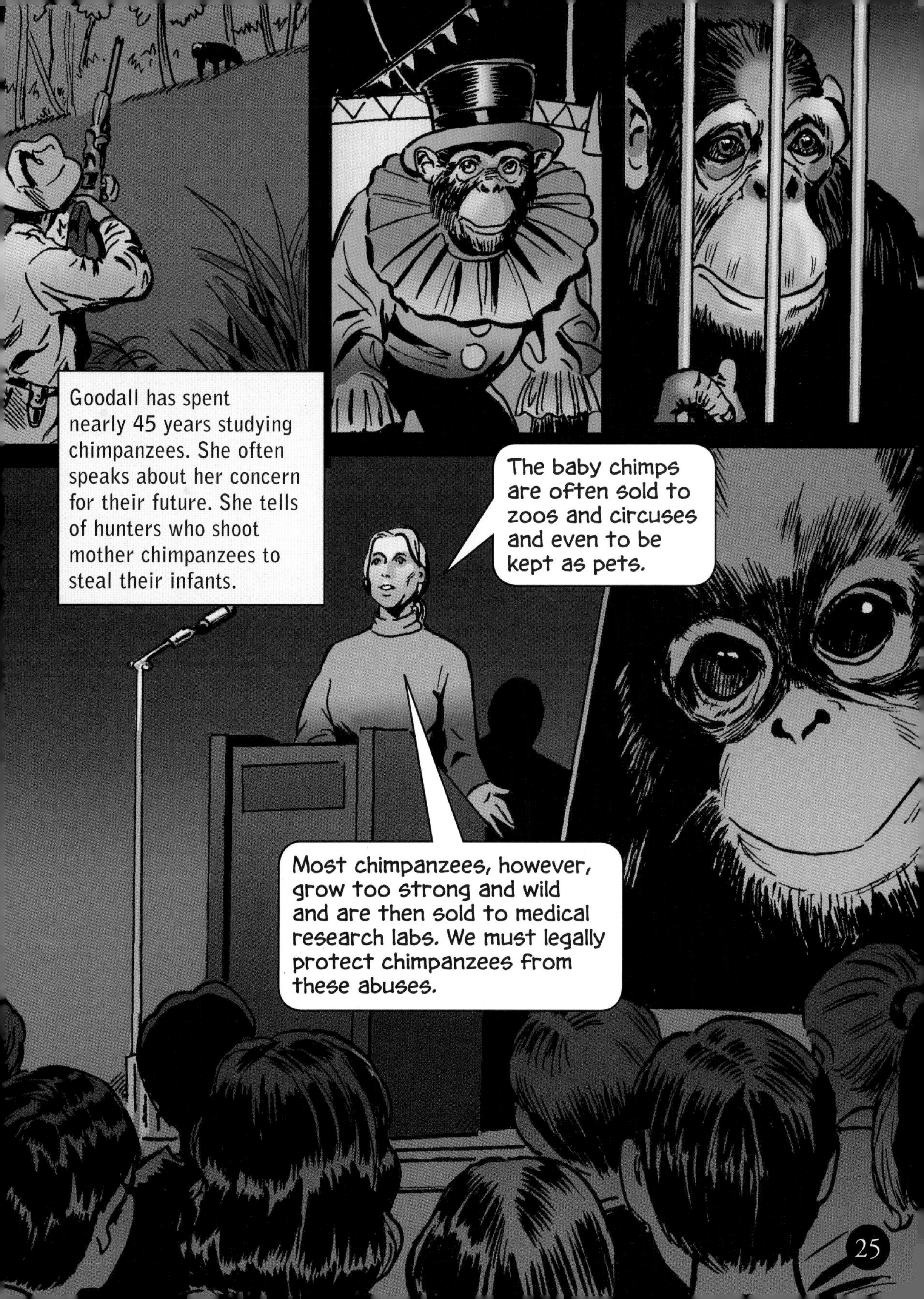

Goodall has spent nearly 45 years studying chimpanzees. She often speaks about her concern for their future. She tells of hunters who shoot mother chimpanzees to steal their infants.
The baby chimps are often sold to zoos and circuses and even to be kept as pets.
Most chimpanzees, however, grow too strong and wild and are then sold to medical research labs. We must legally protect chimpanzees from these abuses.

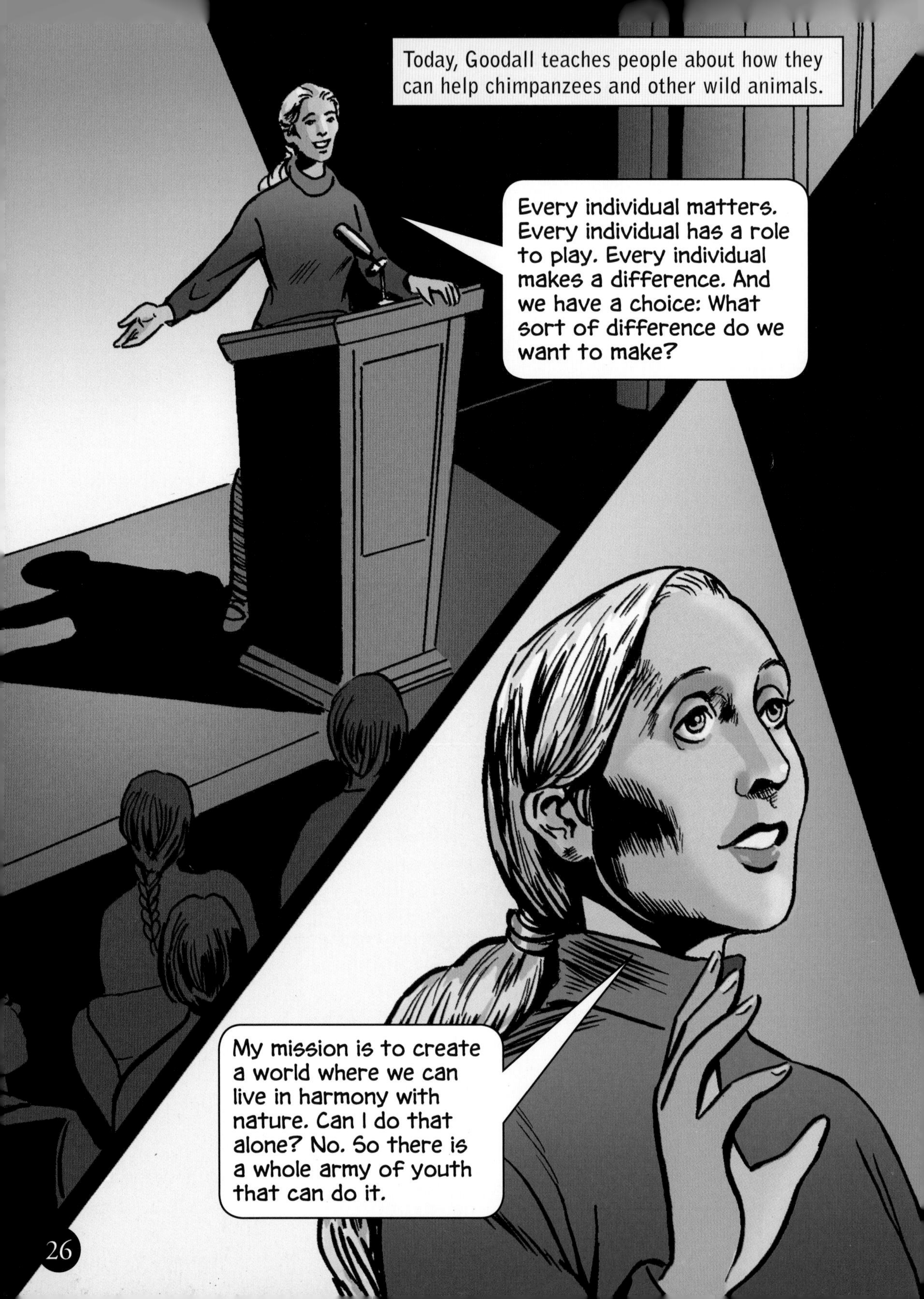
Today, Goodall teaches people about how they can help chimpanzees and other wild animals.
Every individual matters. Every individual has a role to play. Every individual makes a difference. And we have a choice: What sort of difference do we want to make?
My mission is to create a world where we can live in harmony with nature. Can I do that alone? No. So there is a whole army of youth that can do it.

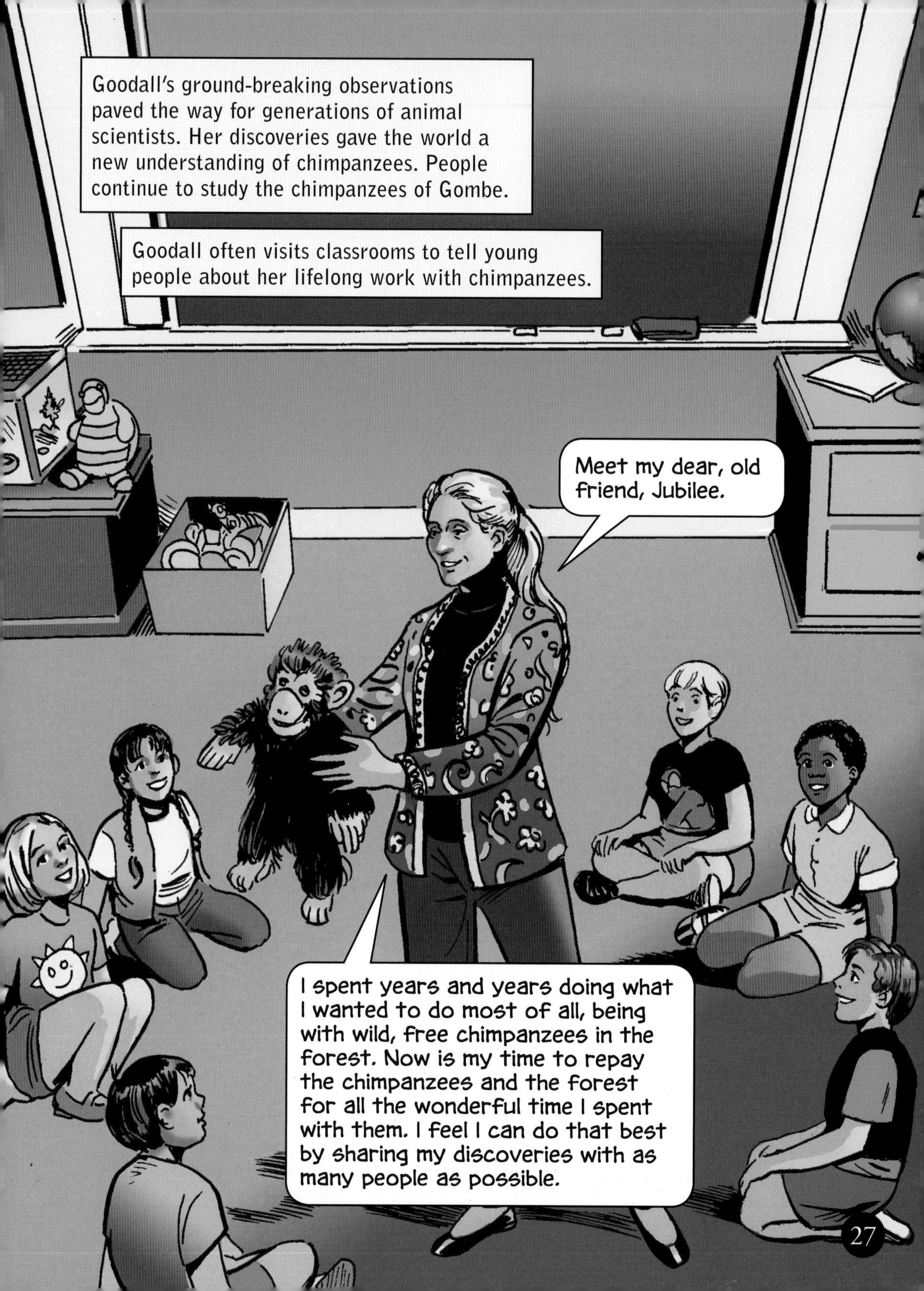
Goodall's ground-breaking observations paved the way for generations of animal scientists. Her discoveries gave the world a new understanding of chimpanzees. People continue to study the chimpanzees of Gombe.
Goodall often visits classrooms to tell young people about her lifelong work with chimpanzees.
Meet my dear, old friend, Jubilee.
I spent years and years doing what I wanted to do most of all, being with wild, free chimpanzees in the forest. Now is my time to repay the chimpanzees and the forest for all the wonderful time I spent with them. I feel I can do that best by sharing my discoveries with as many people as possible.

MORE ABOUT JANE GOODALL

Jane Goodall's full name is Valerie Jane Morris-Goodall. She was born on April 3, 1934, to Mortimer and Margaret Morris Goodall. Her sister, Judy, was born in 1938.

Dangerous animals like crocodiles, snakes, and leopards shared Goodall's African surroundings. With the help of her African guides, she learned how to stay safe from these animals.

Goodall noticed that the chimpanzees were grouped as families. Unlike other scientists, Goodall named, instead of numbered, each chimpanzee. She grouped the individual families by a letter of the alphabet. For example, Flo and Flint were in the same family.

Goodall observed how chimpanzees can be violent and aggressive. Some scientists wanted Goodall to hide her findings. They worried that the new information would show violent behavior in humans is a genetic trait. But Goodall decided to publish her findings.

The Jane Goodall Institute headquarters is in Silver Springs, Maryland. Today, the Institute has offices around the world, including England, China, and Japan.

Goodall has received many awards, including the Kyoto Prize, the Encyclopedia Britannica Award, and the Animal Welfare Institute's Albert Schweitzer Award. She is the only non-Tanzanian to have received the Medal of Tanzania.

Goodall has written articles for many journals and magazines, including National Geographic. She has also written several books, including *Reason for Hope: A Spiritual Journey* and *The Chimpanzees of Gombe: Patterns of Behavior*. She has also written books for young people, such as *The Chimpanzee Family Book* and *My Life With the Chimpanzees*.

The Jane Goodall Institute sponsors the Roots and Shoots program for children. Activities include hands-on projects to teach kids about caring for all living things. Groups plant trees, pick up garbage, and support animal shelters.

GLOSSARY

ethology (eth-OL-uh-jee)—the study of animal behavior

genetic trait (juh-NET-ik TRATE)—a characteristic passed from one generation to the next

harmony (HAR-muh-nee)—to be in agreement

observation (ob-zur-VAY-shuhn)—to carefully watch something

scientist (SYE-uhn-tist)—a person who studies the world around us

termite (TUR-mite)—an antlike insect that eats wood; termites build large mounds, where they live together in colonies.

INTERNET SITES

FactHound offers a safe, fun way to find Internet sites related to this book. All of the sites on FactHound have been researched by our staff.

Here's how:

1. *Visit www.facthound.com*
2. Type in this special code **0736854851** for age-appropriate sites. Or enter a search word related to this book for a more general search.
3. Click on the **Fetch It** button.

FactHound will fetch the best sites for you!

READ MORE

Haugen, Brenda. *Jane Goodall: Legendary Zoologist.*
Signature Lives. Minneapolis: Compass Point Books, 2006.

Kozleski, Lisa. *Jane Goodall.* Women in Science.
Philadelphia: Chelsea House, 2003.

Woronoff, Kristen. *Jane Goodall: Animal Scientist.* Famous
Women. Detroit: Blackbirch Press, 2002.

BIBLIOGRAPHY

Goodall, Jane. *Africa in My Blood: An Autobiography in
Letters: The Early Years.* Boston: Houghton Mifflin, 2000.

Goodall, Jane. *Beyond Innocence: An Autobiography in
Letters: The Later Years.* Boston: Houghton Mifflin, 2001.

Goodall, Jane. *The Chimpanzees I Love: Saving Their World
and Ours.* New York: Scholastic, 2001.

Goodall, Jane. *My Life with the Chimpanzees.* New York:
Pocket Books, 1996.

Goodall, Jane. *Through a Window: My Thirty Years with the
Chimpanzees of Gombe.* Boston: Houghton Mifflin, 1990.

INDEX